JOURNEY
To Freedom

14 - DAY DEVOTIONAL

KATRINA D. SMITH

Journey To Freedom

Copyright © 2022 Katrina D. Smith

All Rights Reserved. All rights reserved. This book or any portion thereof may not be reproduced or used in any manner without the publisher's express written permission except for the use of brief quotations in a book review.

ISBN: 979-8-9855826-3-5

Printed in the USA.

Table of Contents

Introduction *1*

Day One: Freedom *3*

Day Two: Confidence *6*

Day Three: Autonomy *8*

Day Four: Peace *10*

Day Five: Strength *12*

Day Six: Truth *14*

Day Seven: Live *16*

Day Eight: Liberation *18*

Day Nine: Release *21*

Day Ten: Self-Determination *24*

Day Eleven: Independence *27*

Day Twelve: Unhindered *30*

Day Thirteen: Rest *33*

Day Fourteen: Spontaneity *36*

DEDICATION

I'm grateful to God for extending me another opportunity to stretch beyond my comfort zone. I'm so appreciative that He is so mindful of me. Thank you to my family and friends for believing in me. Thank you to my leader, Pastor Shannon L. McRae, for taking the time to mentor and coach me along this journey to freedom. Your selflessness has not gone unnoticed. I truly love and appreciate you all very much!

IN REMEMBRANCE OF

To my beautiful cousins, Jennifer W. Elliott and Tanja T. Britt: You both lived, loved, and laughed without restraint. Thank you for leaving the blueprint on how to live *freely*. I truly miss and love you both so much.

INTRODUCTION

This inspirational journal is about assuring some and reminding others that God's purpose is not for us to live in bondage on any level. His whole purpose for sending His only begotten Son was/is for us to have and live an abundant life freely and cheerfully. So, come on and journey with me for the next 14 days with inspirational writing, scriptures, and prayer to discover, accept, and embrace the *freedom* God has promised us. The Word of God makes it very clear that once we are delivered from a yoke of bondage, we have the power to make sure we don't allow ourselves to be burdened with any yoke of bondage again. *"It is for freedom that Christ has set us free. Stand firm, then, and do not let yourselves be burdened again by a yoke of slavery." Galatians 5:1 NIV*

Are you ready for the challenge? Sure, you are! Let's Go... God's freedom shall be your portion.

DAY ONE

FREEDOM

(noun) the power or right to act, speak or think as one wants without hindrance or restraint.

A major hindrance to living a life of freedom is manipulation. There's nothing worse than feeling trapped in a manipulative situation and can't see your way out. Societal pressures, familial circumstances, and workplace demands are generally situations we face daily. We have a responsibility not only for ourselves but for others. Most of the time, we live our lives to make others comfortable and happy, even at the expense of our happiness. This can easily be a form of manipulation and control to keep people oppressed.

Manipulation is a form of emotional abuse. It has the power to affect the physical, mental, and emotional health of an individual. As quiet as it is kept, the person being manipulated isn't always aware that this is even happening. Victims of manipulation suffer from depression, anxiety, difficulty developing healthy coping skills, lying about their feelings, putting others' needs ahead of their own, and finding it difficult to trust others. At best, manipulation robs people of their freedom of speech and ability to make informed decisions.

The first step on this journey to freedom is to acknowledge areas of bondage or oppression. To be free from this oppression, you must identify the manipulative behavior. Recognize the motives behind the manipulation and disengage from the manipulator. One must resist the temptation to remain in situations in which they've (voluntarily or involuntarily) given control over to another. Anything in your life that you were previously bound to have to be submitted to the Lord in prayer. The journey to freedom can indeed be frightening. Commit to following the Lord, knowing He will always lead you in the right direction.

Think back to when you felt trapped in a situation and God set you free. Once you were free, did you see going back as an option? Hopefully, you did not. Guard your freedom like your life depends on it because it does.

Steps to Breaking Free:

- Put yourself first.
- Set firm boundaries.
- Manage your emotions.
- Trust your judgment.
- Be confident.
- Stop compromising.
- Keep reinventing yourself.

"So, if the Son sets you free, you will be free indeed." - John 8:36 NIV

"It is for freedom that Christ has set us free. Stand firm, then, and do not let yourselves be burdened again by a yoke of slavery." - Galatians 5:1 NIV

"I would like to be remembered as a person who wanted to be free, so other people would also be free." – Rosa Parks.

DAY TWO

~~~

CONFIDENCE

(noun) a feeling or consciousness of one's powers or reliance on one's circumstances.

Do you always have second thoughts or struggle about what to do? Do you try to reconsider a decision after making it? Do you criticize yourself if things don't go as planned? If you answered *yes* to these questions, let's consider your lack of confidence. Although confident people are not immune to self-doubt, they have a strong sense of assurance, clarity, and self-trust. Confidence influences all aspects of your life, including work, ministry, and relationships. Numerous experiences can hurt your confidence, but it's worth making an effort to build it again.

God wants you to have confidence in life! Not bragging or arrogance, but a sure knowledge of who you are in Him! Live your life in a manner that's acceptable to God. You have the freedom to approach God with confidence, understanding that He hears and will answer your prayers. ***"And my God will supply all your need according to His riches in glory by Christ Jesus." – Philippians 4:9 NKJV***

In those moments when you don't feel good enough, strong enough, or incapable, remind yourself of who God says you are!

The Word of God will encourage you and give you the strength to keep going.

Here are several reasons why your confidence matters.

- Being confident can improve your health.
- With confidence, you are not vulnerable to peer pressure.
- Confidence enables you to keep things in perspective.
- Confidence helps to build resiliency.
- Confidence helps you maintain healthy boundaries.

"So, do not throw away your confidence; it will be richly rewarded. You need to preserve so that when you have done the will of God, you will receive that he was promised." - Hebrews 10:35-36 NIV

"For you created my inmost being; you knit me together in my mother's womb. I praise you because I am fearfully and wonderfully made; your works are wonderful, I know that full well." – Psalm 139:13-14 NIV

"Being confident of this, that he who began a good work in you will carry it on to completion until the day of Christ Jesus." - Philippians 1:6

"Your success will be determined by your own confidence and fortitude." – Michele Obama

DAY THREE

AUTONOMY

(noun) freedom from external control or influence; independence.

Have you ever found yourself "walking on eggshells" to avoid conflict? Do you feel the need to check-in or ask permission to do what makes you happy? Do you find yourself apologizing even if you've done nothing wrong? If you answered yes to any of these questions, it's time to figure out who you *really* are.

Nothing screams being held hostage like codependency. Codependency refers to the mental, emotional, physical, or spiritual dependence upon a friend, partner, or family member. Codependent relationships are centered around power that promotes the needs of the taker—leaving the giver in a place of continuous sacrifice. It generally becomes unhealthy when a person loses self-awareness. Losing autonomy occurs when another person takes over the decision-making role in your life.

Common Signs of Codependency Are:

- Constantly seeking validation.
- Your self-worth depends on what other people think.

- Habitually takes on more than you can realistically handle.
- Frequently takes on blame in hopes of keeping the peace.
- Does things you don't want to do to make others happy.
- Have an overwhelming fear of rejection or abandonment.

If you agree that you have experienced any of these unhealthy signs of codependency, you must decide to become more self-reliant. It is time to regain self-control and autonomy. It's okay to state your own needs and desires. If you find yourself struggling, ask for support. On your journey to freedom, you should feel comfortable expressing your needs. Lastly, let others know when they are asking too much of you without worrying about being rejected.

"You, my brothers and sisters, were called to be free. But do not use your freedom to indulge the flesh[a]; rather, serve one another humbly in love. For the entire law is fulfilled in keeping this one command: "Love your neighbor as yourself" - Galatians 5:13-14 NIV

"Autonomy is the whole thing; it's what unhappy people are missing. They have given the power to run their lives to other people." – Judith Guest

Katrina D. Smith

DAY FOUR

PEACE

(noun) a state of tranquility or quiet: such as freedom from disquieting or oppressive thoughts or emotions.

Some years ago, I had a job that became stressful and, at times, extremely overwhelming. I remember praying and asking God for strength, peace of mind, and the ability to handle the workload. Within a couple of months of praying, the Company notified all employees that they would begin laying off workers to reduce expenses. However, not one of us was sure of who would remain employed or who would be laid off. So, the Company began the reduction in force by letting go of contractors, a process that took a couple of weeks. On the day the Company began informing full-time personnel of their status, I was calm and, for some reason, was not worried about the outcome. That same day I was notified that I was being laid off within two weeks. At that moment, I was so relieved. Where I thought God would answer my prayers one way, He answered another way; by releasing me from that job.

I remember one of my coworkers, who was also laid off, was very angry. He approached me and asked if I was upset. And I said, "No, actually I'm not. I'm more relieved than anything because this job was becoming too stressful. And besides, the same God that blessed me with this job will bless me with another one." He looked at me as if he was shocked that I wasn't upset. God has given us the ability to be at peace even during the chaos. No matter what is happening around us, if we submerge ourselves in God's presence, all the noise must cease. Anything that's bothering us must lose its grip on us. We must be intentional daily about keeping our minds on God, and He'll keep us in perfect peace regardless of what we face.

Call to Action: Find a scripture to read and meditate on it throughout the day. Play some inspirational instrument music.

"And the peace of God, which surpasses all understanding, will guard your hearts and your minds in Christ Jesus." - Philippians 4:7 ESV

"Peace I leave with you; my peace I give to you. Not as the world gives do I give to you. Let not your hearts be troubled, neither let them be afraid." - John 14:27

"Peace and friendship with all mankind is our wisest policy, and I wish we may be permitted to pursue it." - Thomas Jefferson

DAY FIVE

～⁓～

STRENGTH

(noun) the quality or state of being strong: capacity for exertion or endurance.

Being strong spiritually and mentally is just as important as being strong physically. In Isaiah 41:10, God instructs us not to be afraid. He promises us that He will help us and strengthen us. You cannot deliver yourself or even win the battles you're going through without God. God never intended for you to fight alone. The enemy's job is to exploit our weaknesses and cause us to rely on everything and everyone other than God. However, God has all power and is our strength. Even on your best day, you will need God's strength. You must know who you are and your purpose. Believing in yourself and trusting God will help you build your spiritual and mental strength. Take time to get to know yourself, to understand your desires, your goals, your weaknesses, and your limits. Look at this as means of becoming a better version of yourself. Reinventing yourself is not impossible if you're willing to put in the work.

Call to Action:

1. Build your faith through prayer, meditation and the Word.

2. Spend time getting to know yourself.

3. Face your fears.

4. Be kind to yourself and others.

5. Practice being grateful, even in difficult situations.

6. Be patient with your growth.

7. Surround yourself with positive-minded people.

8. Choose to eat healthier.

9. Learn to relax and rest.

"Fear thou not; for I am with thee: be not dismayed; for I am thy God: I will strengthen thee; yea, I will help thee; yea, I will uphold thee with the right hand of my righteousness." - Isaiah 41:10 KJV

"Be strong and courageous; do not be frightened and do not be dismayed, for the Lord your God is with you wherever you go." - Joshua 1:9 ESV

"I can do all things through Christ which strengtheneth me." - Philippians 4:13 KJV

"Where there is no struggle, there is no strength." - Oprah Winfrey

DAY SIX

~~~

TRUTH

(noun) sincerity in action, character, and utterance.

Truth is the essence of freedom. The truth is we cannot afford to stay bound. Freedom from past thoughts and unrealistic expectations is true freedom. We must trust God and His Word. We must see ourselves as God sees us. We must not allow the opinions or the unreasonable expectations of others to hold us hostage. Truth is being free from satan's deceptions and lies. Satan is a liar, and he is the father of all lies (John 8:44).

To be free is to experience the joy of God through His Word. His Word is the truth! John 14:6, Jesus saith unto him, I am the way, the truth, and the life: no man cometh unto the Father, but by me. 1 John 5:6 states, "And it is the Spirit who testifies because the Spirit is the truth. Biblical truth is the knowledge of the Law of God and its application, and it keeps us whole. As you journey along to your place of freedom, here are a few more scriptures that remind us of the truth!

We are never alone.
So do not fear, for I am with you; do not be dismayed, for I am your God. I will strengthen you and help you; I will uphold you with my righteous right hand. **– Isaiah 41:10**

God's character remains constant.
Jesus Christ is the same yesterday and today and forever... – **Hebrews 13:8**

God's grace is sufficient.
My grace is sufficient for you, for my power is made perfect in weakness. – **2 Corinthians 12:9**

Christ Made Us New.
Therefore if any man be in Christ, he is a new creature: old things are passed away; behold, all things are become new. **--2 Corinthians 5:17**

Call to Action: Use the Word of God to support the following "I Am" Affirmations.

AFFIRMATION	SUPPORTING SCRIPTURE
I AM HEALED.	
I AM SET FREE.	
I AM FORGIVEN.	
I AM ENOUGH.	
I AM VICTORIOUS.	

Truth is powerful, and it prevails. - Sojourner Truth

DAY SEVEN

~~~

LIVE

(verb) a) having life; b) to continue to have life; remain alive.

It's time for us to LIVE on purpose! Let's not continue to merely exist. No matter what mistakes we have made or what other people have said and done to us, we must make up our minds that we will live as God desires for us to live. There is so much greatness inside of us. God does not want us to just exist. Jesus said He came that we may have life and have it more abundantly (John 10:10b). That abundance will not appear unless we take positive steps to prepare ourselves for the abundant life God has planned for us. We must give God something to work with. I know from experience that our lives must have balance for us to flourish like God wants us to. We must also be obedient and have faith and confidence in God's will for us to prosper and succeed.

We must be disciplined in whatever steps we are taking to better ourselves and our life. And please don't think of discipline as something negative. Think of discipline as doing something we may not want to do but must do so we can see the changes we want. And with being disciplined, we also must be consistent. For example, we cannot work on renewing our minds once a week. We must work on renewing our minds daily. The life God desires for us to live requires us to remain steadfast in His Word and consist in prayer. *Jesus answered, "It is written: Man shall not live on bread alone, but on every word that comes from the mouth of God." Matthew 4:4 NIV.* We cannot live an abundant life apart from God, His Word, and prayer.

If you're going to live and pursuing living a fulfilling life, start by putting these practical pointers to use:

- Know your strengths.
- Learn new skills.
- Be consistent in your pursuit.
- Follow your passions.
- Celebrate your successes.

"The thief cometh not, but for to steal, and to kill, and to destroy: I am come that they might have life, and that they might have it more abundantly." John 10:10 KJV

"The whole point of being alive is to evolve into the complete person you were intended to be." - Oprah Winfrey

DAY EIGHT

~~~

LIBERATION

(noun) the act of setting someone free from imprisonment, slavery, or oppression; release. Freedom from limits on thoughts of behavior.

Being Free starts in your mind! You must first believe that you are free. It's one thing to be oppressed by people; however, it's another thing to be oppressed by your thoughts. We must free our minds from the uninvited guests such as negative thoughts, doubt, fear, and other people's views and replace them with positive thoughts, faith, courage, and God's view according to His Word. Meditation can improve all areas of life. What's on your mind?

 We must take an honest look at ourselves, examine our habits and thoughts, and determine if those habits are toxic or healthy. We must rid ourselves of all patterns that are detrimental to our growth, our maturity, and becoming the very person God purposed for us to be. Bad habits will drain all the life out of us, leading us down a path of destruction. We must surround ourselves with successful people to allow ourselves to develop positive habits to aid us in becoming a better version of ourselves.

To grow, mature, and evolve, we must be willing to renew our minds daily with God's Word and take time to create and engage in activities that will help us change an old nonproductive habit into a new positive habit. Of course, it won't be easy, but if you're determined to be better than you were the day before, you will do what is necessary to be successful in developing habits that are more productive and healthy.

Call to Action:

- Start your day with prayer and meditation—Focus on God. Allow God to settle, refresh you spiritually and mentally, and reveal the plans He has for you for today.

- Use visualization: Mentally prepare by visualizing yourself in situations where you experience positive outcomes.

- Command your day by creating and speaking aloud a positive affirmation. **Example:** Today is going to be an Awesome Day!

- Be accountable: Find someone that you know will be honest with you and will hold you accountable to the plan you have established to develop more productive and healthy habits.

"Now the Lord is the Spirit, and where the Spirit of the Lord is, there is liberty." 2 Corinthians 3:17 KJV

Katrina D. Smith

"For to be free is not merely to cast off one's chains, but to live in a way that respects and enhances the freedom of others." - Nelson Mandela

DAY NINE

~~~

RELEASE

(verb) to relieve from something that confines, burdens, or oppresses. (noun) the act or an instance of liberating or freeing (as from restraint).

If I were you, I wouldn't start my own business; just get a better-paying job. If I were you, I wouldn't go to that ministry. If I were you, I wouldn't go to school right now. Do these statements sound familiar? Of course, they do! We've all at some point been held hostage by the "If I were you" statements. We can no longer allow people's unhealthy opinions to keep us from pursuing better, growing, evolving, and maturing into a better version of ourselves. A lot of times, we are so eager to share what we desire to do and what God is showing us that we share with the wrong people for the sake of someone hearing us. And often, when we share with the wrong people, we end up taking a step back, second-guessing ourselves and God because what those people said was not encouraging at all. So, we must know who to share with, what to share, and from who to receive advice. We must stop being affected by other people's opinions.

Many people have lied against others, who, by the way, are innocent because of jealousy and envy. They did it to embarrass, disgrace, and belittle them before other people. Some of you, like myself, have been falsely accused because of people being jealous of or not understanding God working favorably in our life. It was embarrassing and hurtful to hear the things of which I was falsely accused. So, once I realized the way my life was going was not conducive to the life God desires for me, I made up my mind to follow God's lead. Through prayer and fasting, I began seeking God for direction and instructions on accomplishing what he was revealing to me. And He did! Listen, I even asked Him to help me forgive the false accusers, forgive myself, and to vindicate me from the false accusations. I often reminded myself of Isaiah 54:17 *"**No weapon form against thee shall prosper; and every tongue that shall rise against thee in judgment thou shalt condemn. This is the heritage of the servants of the Lord, and their righteousness is of me, saith the Lord.**"* I had to surrender my situation to God and examine myself to ensure I wasn't holding onto any anger or bitterness. And because I allow God to be God, He vindicated me and helped me to release myself from the false accusations, the embarrassment, and hurt.

We will have to do the same for unrealistic expectations that we have imposed on ourselves and those of other people. We cannot be all things to all people. We cannot live our life based on the unrealistic expectation of others or the ones we have for ourselves. We must live our lives according to the Word of God.

Call to Action:

- Take responsibility for yourselves. Be reminded of whose life you're living.

- Stop comparing yourself to others.

- Let God heal you from embarrassment, other people's opinions, and unrealistic expectations.

- Set clear, healthy boundaries. Express them and expect them to be adhered to.

- Increase your confidence through the Word of God and prayer.

"If we confess our sins, he is faithful and just and will forgive us our sins and purify us from all unrighteousness." 1 John 1:9 KJV

"Therefore, if any man be in Christ, he is a new creature: old things are passed away; behold, all things are become new." 2 Corinthians 5:17 KJV

"I believe that a trusting attitude and a patient attitude go hand in hand. You see, when you let go and learn to trust God, it releases joy in your life. And when you trust God, you're able to be more patient. Patience is not just about waiting for something... it's about how you wait, or your attitude while waiting." - Joyce Meyer

DAY TEN

~~~~

SELF-DETERMINATION

(noun): free choice of one's own acts or states without external compulsion.

You have the right and opportunity to live the way you would like. God desires we live a life that mirrors His Word. A life that's pleasing unto Him and brings Him glory. Being self-determined gives you a great feeling of having control of your choices and life. You, having a desire to grow and mature, helps you to make decisions that will have a positive impact on whatever you set out to accomplish and the people you are around. Evaluating, learning, and applying different skills to develop/improve your self-determination, will help you take control of your choices and life. You'll be able to decide what you want to do in your life and act accordingly. As your level of self-determination develops/improves, your interest, passion, and commitment to the things you do increases, encouraging you not to quit on your goals, dreams, or whatever you want to accomplish. Think about all the times you decided to do something, and after a few days, a few weeks, or even months, you give up. Why? It's because of a lack of determination. Against all odds, you must not give up! So, whether you lack or need to increase your self-determination, now is the time to develop it, improve it, and hold yourself accountable to never giving up until you have accomplished each goal and achieved the success you want.

Here are some pointers on how you can develop strong self-determination or improve your self-determination.

- **Have A Clear Picture of What You Want to Achieve.** Determine what's the result you're expecting; your end goal.

- **Know Your Why.** Knowing your purpose for why you want/need to accomplish the goal(s) and dreams you have. Having a sound understanding and strong sense of what you're doing, you will do whatever it takes to achieve the desired result.

- **Limit Your Choices of Goals/Dreams to Pursue At One Time.** Don't overwhelm yourself by setting and trying to work on too many goals at once. Choose one or two goals to work on diligently. Once you have achieved the outcome, you were expecting to pursue something else.

- **Develop a Passion for What You're Doing.** You must love what you're doing. I have learned this lesson from experience; *pursuing with no passion equals a lack of determination.* If you don't love what you're doing, you will give up, especially if things become challenging in your pursuit.

- **Improving Self-Determination:** Believe that you are capable of having control of your life. Know that you can overcome challenges through prayer, hard work, making good choices, and being consistent.

- **Be Self-Motivated**: Engage in actions that help you set goals and work diligently to accomplish them.

- **Take Responsibility for Your Actions**: Always give yourself credit for your success. However, just as important, admit when you're wrong, when you failed, made a bad decision, believe that you can correct the mistake, and take appropriate action to fix your error.

- **Seek Positive Relationships**: You want to surround yourself with people who will support you, hold you accountable, and always be honest with you. And you must offer the same support, love, and feedback to them.

"And let us not be weary in well doing: for in due season we shall reap, if we faint not." Galatians 6:9;

"Stand firm, and you will win life. Luke 21:19; I can do all things through Christ which strengtheneth me." Philippians 4:13 KJV

"You may not control all the events that happen to you, but you can decide not to be reduced by them." – Maya Angelou

DAY ELEVEN

INDEPENDENCE

(noun) the quality or state of being independent.

Do you consider yourself to be self-sufficient? Are you able to make sounds decision about anything without getting everyone's opinion on what you should do? Are you able to go anywhere alone, like to the movies, shopping, or even lunch, instead of always going with someone? If you answered "Yes" to these questions, then you're independent. However, if you answered "No" to these questions, you are codependent. And you will need to overcome the codependency to live a more independent life.

Being independent or learning to be independent will help you build your confidence, build your self-esteem and help you overcome codependency. It will help you understand and love yourself better and discover your likes and dislikes. Independence will also develop your ability to make good decisions and be self-reliant, giving you the freedom to find your reasons for succeeding. You'll be able to speak up for yourself, setting the tone for how you want to be treated and respected by others. You will be empowered to communicate effectively. You won't rely on other people to make you happy. Your independence will assure you that you can take care of yourself. You will be more self-motivated, sensitive towards others, and optimistic about the fact that You, your life, and your destiny matter. Face it; you are a big deal!

Listed are some steps I found beneficial in my becoming more independent. I encourage you to consider these steps and know that your independence matters in you living a healthier and happy life.

- **Set Healthy Boundaries.** These boundaries will protect you and show others your expectation of how you want them to treat and respect you. Please know that whatever boundaries you set, you first must stick to them for others to respect them.

- **Be Confident in Expressing Your Opinions.** Share what you would like to do instead of just going with whatever everyone else wants to do.

- **Find or Rediscover Healthy Hobbies:** If there is something you would like to do, Do It! If there's something you used to do that made you happy, like going for a walk, start doing it again. You don't need to wait on anyone to go with you. Do it on your own!

- **Seek Out an Accountability Partner:** Make being accountable a part of your daily life. Seek out someone with your best interest at heart who will have no issue being honest with you and will hold you accountable because they want to see you prosper in every area of your life. And you must allow them to hold you accountable.

"Live as people who are free, not using your freedom as a cover-up for evil, but living as servants of God." – 1 Peter 2:16 ESV

"A solid sense of self will help a person to lead a full and happy life." - Kimberly Elise Read

DAY TWELVE

UNHINDERED
Not restrained or held back.

Have you ever wondered why you haven't completed a certain goal, received that promotion, or saved the money you plan to save? Could it be hindering spirits? Yes, hindering spirits! You often hear about mind-binding spirits, the spirit of lust, or the spirit of slothfulness. However, it may not be often you hear about hindering spirits. Hindering spirits operate silently and often in unrevealing ways, wreaking havoc as must as possible. They attack your commitment to God, praying, fasting, and reading the Word. You feel less and less like praying, reading and studying the Word, spending time, and worshiping God. Hindering spirits make you lose all interest in the things of God. They lessen your desire to serve Him. These spirits try to hold you in bondage, delaying and disappointing you, hindering your ability to be obedient.

Hindering spirits can wreak havoc even by attacking those close to you. Their sole purpose is to keep you from receiving what God desires to do in you, do with and for you. He tries to discourage you from seeing yourself the way God does. The enemy feeds you negative thoughts about yourself because he wants to taint your self-image. The bible says the enemy comes to steal, kill and destroy. Anything he can do to take you off course, to distract, delay, disappoint or hinder you, he will do that. Take a moment to evaluate your life. If you see any area where you are constantly repeating the same cycle(s), there is a constant struggle to achieve your goals; you must make up your mind to get in the right posture and right alignment with God! No longer allow the enemy to wreak havoc in your life.

Call to Action:

- **Pray:** Father God, I denounce and renounce the Word curses spoken of my life by myself and others. I ask that you forgive me for believing the enemy lies about who I am, whose I am, and what I'm capable of doing. Please give me the ability and the strength to forgive myself. Father, I declare that the Word curses will not have any power over me and my life. I come into agreement with You and your Word. I commit to only speaking and agreeing with words encouraging me and producing life. I shall live and not die, declaring Your works, Heavenly Father! I thank you for delivering me, healing me, and making me whole. In Jesus' name, I pray! Amen!

- **Replace the negative self-image with the image God Has of You:** Change how you see yourself by allowing God's Word to draw you a new image of who He says you are. You can do all things through Christ who strengthens you. You are more than a conqueror.

- **Read and Meditate on God's Word Daily:** You must spend time in God's Word daily. You must remind yourself of what God is saying about you in His Word. Before you start reading, ask God to give you revelation and understanding of what He is saying to you.

"Pray without ceasing." – 1 Thessalonians 5:17 KJV

"I instruct you in the way of wisdom and lead you along straight paths. When you walk, your steps will not be hampered; when you run, you will not stumble." Proverbs 4:11-12 NIV

"Set your minds on things above, not on earthly things." Colossians 3:2 NIV

"Bravery is the audacity to be unhindered by failures, and to walk with freedom, strength, and hope, in the face of things unknown." – Morgan Harper Nichols

DAY THIRTEEN

REST

(noun) a state of motionless or inactivity.

Getting proper rest is just as important as eating properly and exercising. Proper rest (sleep) improves your overall health, brain performance, your mood and reduces stress. Good, uninterrupted sleep helps you think more clearly, get along easier with others, improve your memory and help you do better at work and school increasing your productivity. The lack of sleep will cause you to be irritable, tired, unfocused, easily frustrated, and stressed. Not getting enough sleep can cause health issues such as obesity or heart disease. It can even diminish the time you spend with God in prayer, reading, and meditating on His Word and worshipping Him. Yes, lack of proper sleep can negatively affect your relationship with God and your ability to serve well in ministry. The National Sleep Foundation guidelines advise that adults need 7 to 9 hours of sleep per night. Proper sleep also helps your mind and body to heal and recover from all that has happened in a day. Peaceful and refreshing sleep enables you to reset spiritually, mentally, emotionally, and physically. It also restores your energy, focus, and motivation.

A lack of sleep can contribute to you have insomnia. Insomnia is a sleep disorder in which a person has difficulty getting sleep or staying asleep for long periods. If you're constantly pushing, working, and getting as little as 2 to 3 hours of sleep daily, you may be experiencing insomnia. Sometimes when we overwork ourselves, pushing ourselves to get more done and get minimum rest, we may have difficulty sleeping once we decide to rest. If this is you, some changes need to be made to ensure that you are properly resting, spending quality time with God, and presenting your best self the next day.

Consider these few steps to getting a better night's sleep.

- **Create a Sleep Schedule:** Determine when you will wind down from the day's hustle. Commit to a time that you'll go to bed each night and the time you'll get up each morning.

- **Commit to a Daily Exercise Schedule:** Choose an exercise of your choice to do a least 30 minutes daily.

- **Take Short Naps:** Take a nap for 45 minutes to 1 hour.

- **Schedule Time to Wind Down:** Read your Bible or another book, watch TV, or listen to soothing instrumental music.

"Come to me, all you who are weary and burdened, and I will give you rest. Take my yoke upon you and learn from me, for I am gentle and humble in heart, and you will find rest for

your souls. 30 For my yoke is easy and my burden is light."
Matthew 11:28 – 30 NIV

"Rest when you're weary. Refresh and renew yourself, your body, your mind, your spirit. Then get back to work." - Ralph Marston

DAY FOURTEEN

SPONTANEITY

(noun) The ability to be natural and sincere in your way of thinking and acting.

Aspontaneous person is free of pretentious action. They are sincere, confident, and full of self-esteem. Spontaneous people are free of other people's opinions. They are who they are indeed. To be spontaneous means you don't have to hide who you are. You have no hidden intentions and are free of any kind of falsehood. Spontaneous people tend to do things impulsively and without planning. They are adventurous and are willing to do something in the spur of the moment.

On this journey to freedom, learn how to listen and trust your intuition. Learn to trust yourself a little more. Be confident in knowing that your ideas matter. Get out of your comfort zone and try new things. Change your routine and stop being so predictable. Clear your schedule and be flexible in your weekly routine. Put some free time on your calendar. There is freedom in discovering new adventures. Don't let anyone discourage you from trying new things, going new places, and meeting new people. Imagine living a more spontaneous life. Think of the heightened excitement in your relationships.

Embrace the joyful fulfillment of letting go of your normal routine. Allow detours and randomness into your life by challenging yourself, your fears, and your doubts. Learn to embrace uncertainty and discomfort as a necessary part of your life. Don't be chained and shackled to your old way of living. Identify key patterns that make you predictable and decide if they are worth changing. Figure out what you want and move towards your new goals. Ask yourself the following: What kind of person would I like to be? What kind of life would I like to live? Which routines are helpful? Which of my daily routines is counterproductive? Now start working towards introducing new routines. These new routines will add a variety to your life! Look for some added excitement, adventure, and joy to your existence.

Now let's be clear, being spontaneous does not mean being reckless. This journey to freedom requires being led by the spirit of God. We must consult God the father for wisdom in all things. "*Asking God, the glorious Father of our Lord Jesus Christ, to give you spiritual wisdom[a] and insight so that you might grow in your knowledge of God.*" Ephesians 1:17 NLT

Tips on Living A More Spontaneous Life:

- Connect with new people.

- Create small habits around gratitude.

- Explore new places in your current city.

- Say Yes when a friend asks you to do something new.

- Go on an impromptu adventure with a friend.
- Take a different route to work.
- Plan a surprise trip without an itinerary.
- Reduce timewasters; stop waiting for the perfect time.

"Being spontaneous is being able to respond with confidence; calmly trusting that whatever the outcome, you will have a positive if challenging experience that will lead to greater self-awareness and success." - Sylvia Clare

Made in the USA
Columbia, SC
17 February 2025